D1552558

SEASONS

you have purpose.
your season is for
a reason!

AB

By

Abigail Boudreaux

Seasons

Copyright © 2020 By Abigail Boudreaux

This book may not be copied or reprinted for commercial gain or profit. No part of this book may be reproduced or transmitted in any form or by any means, electronic or mechanical – including photocopying, recording, or by any information storage and retrieval system, without permission in writing from the publisher.

Foreward

"Although the world is full of suffering, it is also full of overcoming it."

—Helen Keller

I have been her pastor's wife for many years now, and I can confidently say that Abigail Boudreaux is a champion for those pushing back against the darkness. At first glance, this young, delicate cajun beauty seems perfectly untouched by suffering, but trust me, she is a warrior. Abby has battled the darkness, emerging as a beacon of hope, lighting the way for others. From this battlefield, she shares hard-fought lessons that carry messages of power over pity, and that purpose can be found in pain.

Abby is a gifted writer who has already had several articles published and distributed nationally. It is refreshing to hear a clear voice of hope, transparency, and vulnerability from her generation. Her desire to use her experiences and talents to bring others closer to God and their purpose is something to which we should all aspire.

Ralph Waldo Emerson said, *"To learn the most important lessons in life, one must each day surmount a fear."* This devotional allows us to challenge ourselves daily by looking at ourselves in the mirror of God's Word. As you navigate through the various topics, you will begin to see the heartbeat of Jesus. He desires to bring victory for the victim, ministry from mistakes, and fruitfulness from failure. Just like Jesus, Abby gets us to focus on the power in our potential, not the magnitude of our mess.

These empowering words of affirmation, backed with scriptures and crafted into concise, relevant, bite-sized pieces is just what we need in the fast-paced world that continually bombards us with negativity. If you're feeling drained and unsure where to look, you can't go wrong to start with this book!

Shara McKee

A Note from the Author

This is a devotional composed of four weeks. Within each week, you will find six themed daily devotionals. For the seventh day, I have inserted some note-taking pages. I encourage you to use the seventh day to write your thoughts, strategies to help you in your season, or quotes and scriptures from the week that touched you.

If you are a person who cringes at the thought of marking up a perfectly good book, this is your permission to mark it up. Highlight, underline and emphasize the things that speak to you. This book was not written to sit crisp on a shelf but to be utilized as a tool of encouragement to help you grow and also motivate you in whatever season you may be in. So highlight, write thoughts, bend the pages if you have too. This is *for you.*

Many of these devotionals were written on a tiny blue couch in the middle of nap time (sometimes on colored construction paper) at a daycare I used to be employed at. But each one of these devotionals is written out of a place of my own growth. It is my prayer for you that whatever season you are in or the challenges you're facing, you will find peace, fulfillment, and a fortress of shelter to be able to endure the pruning, the rain, the wind, and the process of your season.

—**AB**

Table of Contents

INTRODUCTION

To everything, there is a season... Seasons of yes, seasons of no, seasons of darkness, seasons of light, seasons of plenty, and seasons of drought.

It is easy to talk about those easy, good, prosperous seasons but not so easy to talk about the dark, dry, lonely, questioning seasons. The seasons that break our heart, shake our faith, and challenge our intentions as followers of Christ.

Especially as a body of Christ, who is supposed to be crushing darkness and celebrating light. But what we often forget is that those painful hard-to-face, hard-to-acknowledge seasons are typically the time when most of our growth occurs. The thing is, we have to move *through* them. Getting stagnate, discouraged, and lost in these hard seasons is what results in poor decisions, a quitters mentality, harsh questioning, bitterness, and long-lasting symptoms such as anxiety, worry, insecurity, and depression.

It is so incredibly easy to fall, to experience the ache to give up, to make mistakes, but don't beat yourself up, Friend. It's just a part of your pruning season. Through the pain and discomfort, you will find beauty in the heartache at the end of everything.

It is my hope and prayer that this devotional will help you navigate the waters of your hard seasons and also help you come out of it a conqueror.

Your season is for a reason.

"To everything, there is a season and a time to every purpose under the heaven:

A time to be born, and a time to die; a time to plant, and a time to pluck up that which is planted;

A time to kill, and a time to heal; a time to break down, and a time to build up;

A time to weep, and a time to laugh; a time to mourn, and a time to dance;

A time to cast away stones, and a time to gather stones together; a time to embrace, and a time to refrain from embracing;

A time to get, and a time to lose; a time to keep, and a time to cast away;

A time to rend, and a time to sew; a time to keep silence, and a time to speak;

A time to love, and a time to hate; a time of war, and a time of peace."

—Ecclesiastes 3:1-8 KJV

Seasons of Heaviness

BEAUTY FOR ASHES

When you think about 'heaviness,' it's common to think about things in the realm of depression. While that is a part of it, depression is not the only thing that is heavy or has the potential of weighing us down. The grief of certain circumstances, the daily crosses we bear, burdens, sin, hurt, and even our thought life can open the door to a season of heaviness.

Symptoms of heaviness include loneliness, oppression, deep despair, and even feeling like you live under a suffocating cloud of darkness. Heaviness can be a faith quencher, a love stealer, and a deceitful foe. In seasons of heaviness, it's so easy to lose yourself amongst the ashes of your lost hope. But amidst the ashes, it is key to remember that this is a season. The beauty of a season is that it is going to change. You don't have to live here, but you do have the ability to make it your home with your thought life and actions.

Don't allow yourself to be deceived in this season. Don't let the ashes of what used to be trick you out of what could be. You have a Father who can turn the ashes, the dead things, the hurt feelings, or sadness into beauty and joy.

Despite your surroundings, don't let insecurity and hopelessness whisper negative thoughts into your ear. You are loved, you are still chosen, your hope comes from the Lord, and you are not alone. It feels like a hopeless endeavor to seek after things of positivity, of purpose, and even of pleasure when you are surrounded by the exact opposite.

It becomes very discouraging when the cloak of heaviness seems like it will never leave. It is also a very dangerous season if you decide to pitch your tent in the valley of despair. I know it seems grim right now and all you see is piles of ash, but Friend, keep holding on. Keep pushing through what feels impossible. The Lord intends for us to be trees whose roots are planted deep in righteousness.

What you sow in tears, you will reap in joy. He will turn this mourning into joy. You may cry yourself to sleep, feeling overwhelmed with all the ashes but joy will come in the morning. Hold on to this morning with faith because a new day is coming. A season of joy is approaching but you must not give up.

"To appoint unto them that mourn in Zion, to give unto them that mourn in Zion, to give unto them beauty for ashes, the oil of joy for mourning, the garment of praise for the spirit of heaviness; that they might be called trees of righteousness, the planting of the Lord, that he might be glorified."

Isaiah 61:3 KJV

"They that sow in tears shall reap in joy."

Psalm 126:5 KJV

BROKENNESS

At times, we tend to tread upon the topic of brokenness so gently. When we do, it becomes easy for us to detach the deep anguish that accompanies it. It's a human thing to do. Life has a way of distracting us, and we have the tendency to avoid thinking about things that hurt.

It's funny how though circumstances are different, brokenness is still the same. You don't have to go through the same thing as your neighbor to relate to that despair. Circumstances may not be common, but other factors are. A not so obvious and rather common denominator among brokenness is our grief.

Most of the time, brokenness is a hurt combined with anguish and grief over what you lost. Such as a marriage, a son, a daughter, your innocence, your purity, or even a repercussion of a bad decision. Even the misplacement of purpose that God ordained for your life.

Sometimes, it's not so easy to identify what grieves us because of the intense internal pain. And that's okay. It's all part of the grief process—shock, denial, confusion, rejection, frustration, misunderstanding... unable to grasp reality. Don't beat yourself up because you can't pull yourself out of this misery immediately. Sit and cry for a while. Scream a little bit; it is okay. But know, this opens the door for things bigger than a "process." Such things include mind games, depression, anxiety, and bitterness.

I know it's hard, but be careful with emotions associated with your brokenness. If they aren't dealt with properly, they will control you, instead of you controlling them. You are powerful despite your brokenness and equipped to deal with the tactics of the enemy amid your pain.

As you go throughout your day today, I encourage you to have an open conversation with Him about your pain. Find a scripture that you can combat your chaotic thought life with and reach out to someone because just like you, someone out there is also struggling with an inner pain they do not understand. One of the best remedies to take your mind off of your situation is by helping someone else who is struggling.

Friend, I know it hurts now, but it will get better. If you can learn to trust the Creator with your brokenness in this season, you will be able to trust Him in every season.

"The LORD is near to those who have a broken heart and saves those that have a contrite spirit. Many are the afflictions of the righteous, But the LORD delivers him out of them all. He guards all his bones; Not one of them is broken. Evil shall slay the wicked, and those who hate the righteous shall be condemned. The LORD redeems the soul of His servants, and none of those who trust in Him shall be condemned."

Psalms 34:18-22 NKJV

"The lowly he sets on high, and those who mourn are lifted to safety."

Job 5:11 NIV

"I remain confident of this: I will see the goodness of the LORD in the land of the living. Wait for the LORD; be strong and take heart and wait for the LORD."

 Psalm 27:13-14 NIV

WEIGHT OF THE CROSS

I want you to understand this. Life is worth living. Don't let your thoughts, circumstances, or even others, convince you that it's not. I know life can seem impossible. Sometimes things don't get better. And let's be honest; walking this narrow path with a cross on your shoulder isn't easy.

It's sacrificial, it's emotional, and it's intentional. The nature of this walk alone is enough to make those who struggle with control and impulsivity a difficult one to journey.

One of our Christian directives as followers of Christ is to pick up our cross and follow Him. This aspect of our journey, going through life with a cross on our shoulder, is often talked about. But something rarely talked about is the weight of the cross. It's heaviness.

Can we take a minute to acknowledge that this weight can be hard to carry? Especially for those with a melancholy nature. You aren't supposed to claim or live in a depressed state. But it is important to recognize that some personalities are built that way. Even personalities that aren't will, at some point, have depressive moments.

It's okay to be honest with yourself and God when the weight of your cross seems too much to carry. When you feel like throwing in the towel and calling it quits. Maybe you have dropped it, put it down, failed, or even fallen. You may not even feel strong enough to pick it back up again. But I want to encourage you. It is worth picking up again if you can manage to push through the condemnation the enemy has thrown at you for being human. It is worth pushing through, worth picking back up, and worth living for.

Give Him a chance to take part in your burden of heaviness. He, too, had moments of weakness when He was faced with carrying His cross. When you feel like crumbling under the weight, don't forget about the One who carried His cross, so it would be easier for you to carry yours. Life is worth living because He lived.

"Then cometh Jesus with them unto a place called Gethsemane, and saith unto the disciples, Sit ye here, while I go and pray yonder. And he took with him Peter and the two sons of Zebedee and began to be sorrowful and very heavy. Then saith he unto them, My soul is exceeding sorrowful, even unto death: tarry ye here, and watch with me. And he went a little farther, and fell on his face, and prayed, saying, O my Father, if it is possible, let this cup pass from me: nevertheless, not as I will, but as thou wilt."

Matthew 26:36-39 KJV

"Fear not, for I am with you; be not dismayed, for I am your God. I will strengthen you, yes, I will help you, I will uphold you with My righteous right hand."

Isaiah 41:10 NKJV

"Then He said to them all, "If anyone desires to come after Me, let him deny himself, and take up his cross daily, and follow Me. For whoever desires to save his life will lose it, but whoever loses his life for My sake will save it. For what profit is it to a man if he gains the whole world, and is himself destroyed or lost? For whoever is ashamed of Me and My words, of him the Son of Man will be ashamed when He comes in His own glory, and in His Father's, and of the holy angels. But I tell you truly, there are some standing here who shall not taste death till they see the kingdom of God."

Luke 9:23-27 NKJV

GET SOME GRIT

Grit, according to Webster's dictionary means, "firmness of mind or spirit: unyielding courage in the face of hardship or danger."

Grit isn't pleasant to exercise but Friend, we need to get some if we are to navigate these seasons. Especially in seasons that we are so weighed down and it seems impossible for us to ever get back up. It is in the moments of ultimate defeat that we must access the untapped vault of grit.

Strength and courage seem impossible to tap into when you can't grasp beyond your reality. Don't let your darkness blind you... you are still in control. You have the power over, depression, anxiety, worry, fear, and insecurity. Every negative thought that plagues your mind, you have authority over it.

I know, it's challenging. It takes every ounce of will that you can muster. It's hard to be positive when you feel negative. It's hard to force yourself into the light when you have been made accustomed to darkness. It's hard to walk in unconditional love when you feel burdened. I get it.

Friend, creating a standard of get-up-and-go in the face of any difficulty is necessary for your success. It is difficult to face opposition. But if we wait until we feel like we can create some grit, we would always be living in a funk.

Your thoughts are the gateway to your emotions. It must start with your thought life. To change a thought, you must recognize and challenge it with the word of God. If you feel sad, combat it with joy. If you feel hopeless, combat it with purpose. If you feel weak, combat it with the strength of the Lord.

You are allowed to be free from the prison that your emotions pushed you into. You have the power, the strength, and all the tools needed to push them back. You have the authority to tread on serpents and hurtful emotions.

It's time to have a conversation with your mind and spirit. You can get through this. All you need is a little bit of grit and a whole lot of Jesus.

"Casting down imaginations, and every high thing that exalteth itself against the knowledge of God, and bringing into captivity every thought to the obedience of Christ;"

2 Corinthians 10:5 KJV

"Finally, brethren, whatsoever things are true, whatsoever things are honest, whatsoever things are just, whatsoever things are pure, whatsoever things are lovely, whatsoever things are of good report; if there be any virtue, and if there be any praise, think on these things."

Philippians 4:8 KJV

"For as he thinketh in his heart, so is he: Eat and drink, saith he to thee; but his heart is not with thee."

Proverbs 23:7 KJV

"Why art thou cast down, O my soul? and why art thou disquieted within me? hope thou in God: for I shall yet praise him, who is the health of my countenance, and my God."

Psalm 42:11 KJV

HEAVY GRATITUDE

Depression is no respecter of persons. It plagues the middle-aged, the seasoned saints, and even children. The preteens, teenagers, and young adults. In church and out of the church, for short periods or long periods. Whether it be a medical issue, spiritual, or situational, it is real, it is dark, and it is suffocating.

We would be foolish if we don't recognize that people of any age, gender, and religion, at some point, struggle with this weight. It steals your motivation, your light, and your hope. When it is not appropriately dealt with, it will also steal your faith. It can be daunting and overwhelming because of timidity or shame to locate the tools that are needed to beat it. It is okay to admit that you may not have the wherewithal to help yourself.

But that's why I am here. There are various ways to combat triggers for depression.

The following are a few attainable goals to start you on the right path.

First, you need to tell someone where you are and how you are feeling. Get someone who can check on you, pray for you when you can't, and be an accountability partner. This is key, especially in times when you can't help yourself.

Second, be full of gratitude. This is where your grit comes into play. Make a list of everything that you are thankful for. Repeat it over, over and over again until you believe it. Start with being thankful that you woke up this morning. Rerouting your hopeless thoughts into thankful ones will help lift that heavy dark cloud. Your feelings will follow your thoughts. Think of heavy gratitude instead of heavy hopelessness.

Third, pray. Pray when you don't feel like it. Pray when you feel like you can't reach heaven. Find a scripture that you can repeat in your prayers when you can't find the words to express yourself. Find a prayer template. It is okay, as long as you are praying. Like in all things, prayer is essential.

Keep your head up, Friend. He wants to walk with you in your valleys more than in your mountaintops.

"Rejoice always, pray without ceasing, in everything give thanks; for this is the will of God in Christ Jesus for you."

I Thessalonians 5:16-18 NKJV

"I waited patiently for the LORD; And He inclined to me, And heard my cry. He also brought me up out of a horrible pit, Out of the miry clay, And set my feet upon a rock, And established my steps. He has put a new song in my mouth— Praise to our God; Many will see it and fear, And will trust in the LORD."

Psalms 40:1-3 NKJV

"Blessed be the God and Father of our Lord Jesus Christ, the Father of mercies and God of all comfort, who comforts us in all our tribulation, that we may be able to comfort those who are in any trouble, with the comfort with which we ourselves are comforted by God."

11 Corinthians 1:3-4 NKJV

THE DEATH WEIGHT

I realize that talking about sin, shortcomings, and mistakes is an unpopular conversation. But, you will not be able to live fully in your God-given freedom from sin if we don't acknowledge that even the most sanctified among us sin.

Sin is heavy. Romans 6:23 says, "For the wages of sin is death..." No wonder it feels so heavy. It's associated with death. But the beauty of it is, it doesn't have to end in death. The verse continues to say, "... but the gift of God is eternal life through Christ Jesus." The weight of sin may feel like it is choking the life out of you, but our Savior defeated death already. On a hill called Calvary.

It is the ultimate love story. And while we are here, *He still loves you.* Whether you made a bad decision when you were 7 or 47, if you were in church or out of church, He still loves you! He still has a purpose for you. He is not through with you yet because you are a divine project.

Heaviness doesn't always lie within our lack of acceptance of His forgiveness but in us not forgiving ourselves. I know this can be redundant, but you are not perfect. Even when you are walking in your fulfilled purpose, you still won't be perfect. You will still make mistakes and fall quite a few times.

Everyone has secrets, everyone has skeletons left untouched, and everyone struggles with some kind of sin. Give yourself space for grace. Better yet, allow yourself to fail. Take the hand of self-inflicted condemnation off of yourself. This is a fixable mess-up.

While we are flesh, we don't have to live under the burden of our imperfect flesh. The key is not to put yourself in a burdensome prison of shame because of your shortcomings. It is not His will, nor His wish for you to live bound. Even in the middle of your mess, your secrets, your shame, He will still leave the 99 just for you, because He loves you. He commends His perfect, selfless, sacrificial, unfathomable love towards you every single moment. There is nothing too big, too small, or too bad to change His opinion of you.

"But God commendeth his love toward us, in that, while we were yet sinners, Christ died for us."

Romans 5:8 KJV

"I, even I, am he that blotteth out thy transgressions for mine own sake, and will not remember thy sins."

Isaiah 43:25 KJV

"If we confess our sins, he is faithful and just to forgive us our sins, and to cleanse us from all un-righteousness."

1 John 1:9 KJV

"Let us therefore come boldly unto the throne of grace, that we may obtain mercy, and find grace to help in time of need."

Hebrews 4:16 KJV

NOTES

NOTES

Seasons of Fear

FEARFUL

One of the things that took me years to realize is that fear comes in many shapes, many sizes, and many forms. Sometimes fear is subtle, and sometimes it is bold and suffocating. As a child, fear will come in the form of a monster in your closet that appears when the lights go dim. As an adult, fear can come in the form of panic attacks, paranoia, and worry. Fear will latch on to your insecurities or uncertainties. Even the curveballs that are part of life. Let's be honest, sometimes even as an adult, we can feel the lurking of things unseen as we did as children, just like the monster in the closet.

Like many other things, the enemy tries to trip us up; fear is no respecter of person, age, or gender. Perhaps new seasons trigger different kinds of fear. But the intent of fear is the same. To distract us from the purpose God has created us for, to isolate and to destroy. If we are being real in any scenario, fear is debilitating. It scares us. Without knowledge of the resources, tools, and the power that lives inside of us to overcome fear, we are left in a state of fearfulness.

Despite its many faces and forms, there is one thing that all these different quirks of fear have in common. Behind the face of every fear lies a very real, very recognizable spirit. However, if the spirit of fear has a hold on your life, you have the power to take hold of it. The Bible says that He has not given us a spirit of fear, but one of power, love, and a sound mind. It is not His will for you to be struggling with this frightful spirit. Fear is a tactic of the darkness waring after our soul. But the light that lives inside of you can squash every tactic and fear in every season.

"I sought the LORD, and he answered me: he delivered me from all my fears."

Psalm 34:4 KJV

"The LORD is my light and my salvation— whom shall I fear? The LORD is the stronghold of my life— of whom shall I be afraid?"

Psalm 27:1 KJV

"For I am persuaded, that neither death, nor life, nor angels, nor principalities, nor powers, nor things present, nor things to come, nor height, nor depth, nor any other creature, shall be able to separate us from the love of God, which is in Christ Jesus our Lord."

Romans 8:38-39 KJV

THE TRUST THIEF

If you were able to view a slideshow of thoughts that you have in a single day, how many of those slides would be slides of worry?

Worry is such an integrated part of our human processes that it almost seems unharmful. There is always something to worry about and stress out over. Kids growing up and into new phases. Bills, college loans, worrisome diagnosis, deadlines that seem impossible. Or worse, worrying about where your next meal will come from, or how you will put clothes on your babies' backs.

It easy to worry. It's a natural human emotion. I hate to break it to you, but did you know the situation you are worried about is not the enemy in this equation? It's your worry.

Worrying, stressing, and fretting, that's your enemy. It's the thief that comes to steal your peace and leaves anxiety in its place. More importantly, it steals the trust you have in your Provider, who is your heavenly Father. Worrying forces you to dwell on the negativity in your life and putting a stock on material things or human provision.

I know how easy it is to get ahead of yourself and feel overwhelmed by things that life throws at us. We all have worries uniquely tailored to what life has handed us. But you have to walk in peace knowing that you have a heavenly Father who cares and provides for your every financial, mental, personal, and relational need. Don't forget that your Provider is also the Creator of all our earthly sources.

Friend, you aren't a terrible human being for worrying. But I want to remind you that your source doesn't come from the things of this world, but from the blessing, provision, and protection of God. He is your healer, not your earthly doctor. He is your source of income, not your earthly employer. He is the Protector of your child that has strayed away. He is the supplier, mender, waymaker, and peace giver. He is whatever you need Him to be.

Talk to Him and let Him be what you need Him to be. Trust Him; you are safe living in His arms.

"Therefore, I tell you, do not worry about your life, what you will eat or drink; or about your body, what you will wear. Is not life more than food, and the body more than clothes? Look at the birds of the air; they do not sow or reap or store away in barns, and yet your heavenly Father feeds them. Are you not much more valuable than they? Can any one of you by worrying add a single hour to your life? "And why do you worry about clothes? See how the flowers of the field grow. They do not labor or spin. Yet I tell you that not even Solomon in all his splendor was dressed like one of these. If that is how God clothes the grass of the field, which is here today and tomorrow is thrown into the fire, will he not much more clothe you—you of little faith? So do not worry, saying, 'What shall we eat?' or 'What shall we drink?' or 'What shall we wear?' For the pagans run after all these things, and your heavenly Father knows that you need them. But seek first his kingdom and his righteousness, and all these things will be given to you as well. Therefore do not worry about tomorrow, for tomorrow will worry about itself. Each day has enough trouble of its own."

Matthew 6:25-34 NIV

"Trust in the LORD with all your heart and lean not on your own understanding; in all your ways submit to him, and he will make your paths straight."

Proverbs 3:5-6 NIV

41

PERFECT LOVE

Have you ever had a panic attack? They aren't fun, are they? If you have never had one, I am thankful that you haven't.

Over the years, panic attacks have been labeled many things. I have also heard them referred to as nothing more than an overreaction. But in this day in age, it is ignorant to dismiss panic attacks and anxiety as overreacting or being too sensitive, especially with so many accessible tools to learn about its quirks.

Anxiety can be triggered by all sorts of things. Big crowds, new environment, changes, feeling like you are alone, feeling out of control, and the list goes on. Some live with having anxiety disorders and others experience situational anxiety. We all, at some point will go through a time of being anxious. Unfortunately, sometimes that anxiousness can turn into more severe instances of panic attacks.

I don't know where you are at right now or the kind of anxieties that you are facing, but it is going to be okay. You are going to be fine. The motivator behind anxiety is fearfulness or worry. The Bible says that perfect love casts out all fear.

The word love in that verse is referring to the Greek word agape. Agape is the kind of love that God shows us. It is the highest form of love, and wide open in its action. Agape love is what we should call perfect love. It's the love that died for you, continues to be poured out on you, and doesn't expect anything in return.

You have access to a God who loves you with a perfect love. Agape love defeated the fear and anxiousness you feel, on a hill called Calvary.

Anxiety and panic are just tactics that our enemy uses to steal our peace and derail us from our purpose. As long as the enemy keeps you fretting, doubting, and worrying, he will have your attention. But if you set your mind on the truth and power of God's love, it will push out the enemy's access to your mind and feelings.

The next time you feel your heart pounding, breath shortening, and the weight of incessant worry, take a minute. Breathe, remind yourself of God's love and provision. Start quoting scriptures that disarm the power of fear. The God of love who dwells inside of you and lives all around you casts out fear. You only need to take that fear to Him.

"There is no fear in love; but perfect love casts out fear, because fear involves torment. But he who fears has not been made perfect in love."

1 John 4:18 NIV

"In the multitude of my anxieties within me, Your comforts delight my soul."

Psalm 94:19 NKJV

"Cast your burden on the Lord, and he shall sustain you; he shall never permit the righteous to be moved."

Psalm 55:22 KJV

"Whenever I am afraid, I will trust You."

Psalm 56:3 NKJV

THE REJECTED SOUL

One of my weak points growing up was being vulnerable enough to show authentic love for God. My introverted personality made me believe that I would never be able to connect with people like my extroverted friends because of my convictions. For a long time, "soul-winning" or "sharing the gospel" was intimidating to me. I settled for a comfortable conclusion that my calling was to connect with people through writing, and not the traditional face-to-face interaction.

As I got older, graduated high school, and made my way into a secular workforce, I began to realize that I used my personality and convictions as an excuse of why I felt like I couldn't connect with people. It became evident that it was an intense fear of rejection that bled over into more than just my work life. When I began to uncover this truth, it was as if a whole book unfolded before me of how this fear dictated, and habitually formed how I created and kept relationships. I patterned my life around this fear of rejection, and I didn't realize it.

Being afraid of rejection is such a confining box to be in. If you live there too long, those walls will be solidified. It will steal your freedom and take away your ability to walk in your only true commission to love people and share this truth. Living a separated life is intimidating at times (even inside the church), but the distinct difference is what draws those who are hungry.

It's a process to break out of this fear, but something to keep in mind is that being rejected is inevitable. But it is such a small sacrifice compared to the rejection that He endured for you. If you can look back and try to locate the root of what triggered you into this season, when you do, you will be able to properly disarm this fear. Start dismissing the lies planted in your mind now.

You can be a witness and share your testimony. You are made uniquely to do the work God has called you to do and reach the souls he has ordained for you to reach. You are not meant to be a spectator of the harvest, but a seed planter.

Friend, you are capable of healthy relationships. God will send you the friends you need that will lift and embrace your quirks. We are all human, so we are not free of error. Even your closest friends can reject you indirectly. But you can work through it.

Above all, God will never reject you. He is always accepting every one of your quirks and shortcomings.

He made you; He knows your quirks better than you do. He is ready to help you disarm this fear.

"Jesus saith unto them, Did ye never read in the scriptures, The stone which the builders rejected, the same is become the head of the corner: this is the Lord's doing, and it is marvelous in our eyes?"

Matthew 21:42 KJV

"If the world hate you, ye know that it hated me before it hated you."

John 15:28 KJV

"Go ye therefore, and teach all nations, baptizing them in the name of the Father, and of the Son, and of the Holy Ghost: Teaching them to observe all things whatsoever I have commanded you: and, lo, I am with you always, even unto the end of the world. Amen."

Matthew 28:19-20 KJV

"Be sober, be vigilant; because your adversary the devil, as a roaring lion, walketh about, seeking whom he may devour:"

1 Peter 5:8 KJV

THE MONSTER IN THE CLOSET

She awoke in a panic. Fear cradled her as if she was his baby. She was his now. He claimed all ownership the day she abandoned her prayers. She gave him an inch, and he took her life. Fear not only haunts her in suns light but now even in the moon's light. Her days are rocked with paranoia, and her thoughts are becoming less her own. He was always there. Pouncing, preying, and feasting on a life that had a purpose. But oh, if she only really knew. She could feel him laughing and taunting, convinced that he was laughing because she felt she had no control. But in reality, he was laughing at how naive she was. This girl was powerful, strong, anointed, a leader, a person who didn't see her potential. Fear knew that and also realize how small and weak he is. He mocks her lack of faith, her doubt for Almighty God.

Even as an adult, sometimes fear can just be like that. Fear is similar to the monster under your bed or hiding in your closet. Except, this kind of fear isn't hiding anywhere, rather it causes you to hide in the closet or under the bed. It's irrational, but it's real. Oh, so real.

Your enemy will use every tactic necessary to throw you off course, or to (quite literally sometimes) scare you away from what God has for you. Through nightmares or a lingering feeling of panic as you go about your day to day duties, fear is very real. It steals your sleep, your peace, and freedom to live fully in the God of peace.

I just wanted you to know that you are in good company. Battling with fear doesn't make you childlike. I dare to say that it makes you very Godlike. If the enemy is throwing fear at you, then he must be scared senseless, afraid of who God has made you to be.

I know how hard it is to function under this kind of fear. I understand how impossible it is to utter a prayer. But let me tell you a little secret. Speaking the name of Jesus is more than sufficient. All the power of your deliverance lies in His name.

This season will end, and you will come out victorious. Just hold on a little bit longer. Your redeemer liveth. The God of peace will crush the enemy of fear under your feet. You only need to say His name, Jesus.

"Peace I leave with you, my peace I give unto you: not as the world giveth, give I unto you. Let not your heart be troubled, neither let it be afraid."

John 14:27 KJV

"Thou wilt keep him in perfect peace, whose mind is stayed on thee: because he trusteth in thee."

Isaiah 26:3 KJV

"I will both lay me down in peace, and sleep: for thou, Lord, only makest me dwell in safety."

Psalm 4:8 KJV

"Great peace have they which love thy law: and nothing shall offend them."

Psalm 119:165 KJV

DEATH OF PURPOSE

I don't know what is worse. Wondering, and seeking for your purpose, or knowing your purpose and being afraid of achieving it. Not having a clue may cause a bit of unease. But knowing it, afraid of it or not, you become responsible for what that purpose entails.

The enemy wants nothing more but to destroy you and those who will be touched by your personalized ministry. He will stop at nothing to bring up every flaw or incapability and rub it in your face until you believe you are incapable.

But remember, Moses had a speech impediment. David was a shepherd. Mephibosheth was a cripple. Abraham and Sarah couldn't have children. Gideon was fearful. Jonah ran away. Esther was a Jew. Abigail was married to a drunk. The list is endless of people who had uncomfortable and impossible obstacles to overcome in the face of fulfilling their purpose.

Let me share a personal moment with you; resisting, or running away from the visions, burdens, and passions that God has given you will only leave you unsatisfied and struggling to maintain a relationship with God. I understand that what God may want you to do seems way out of your comfort zone, personality type, and even social status, but He does not call the equipped. He equips the called.

He assures us through His word that He will not give us more than we can bear. He will not send you overseas overnight or put you in front of crowds before you are ready. He is carefully strengthening, encouraging, nudging, and guiding your every step along this daunting journey filled with detours and roadblocks.

The ball is in your court. If you have been privileged to get a glimpse of your purpose, it is up to you to choose to be among the chosen. If you don't know and you are losing hope to the fact that you have a purpose, remember that our first purpose is to be a witness and share this truth with others. So, talk to a coworker, a family member, a cashier at the grocery store, etc. Show yourself friendly and spread the love of God despite not knowing, or if you are having doubts about your purpose.

Don't be afraid of your future. But trust in the Father who holds your future. He won't let you down, and He will never let you go. You can do this. You are capable of fulfilling your purpose every single day.

"Have I not commanded you? Be strong and courageous. Do not be afraid; do not be discouraged, for the LORD your God will be with you wherever you go."

Joshua 1:9 KJV

"David also said to Solomon his son, "Be strong and courageous, and do the work. Do not be afraid or discouraged, for the LORD God, my God, is with you. He will not fail you or forsake you until all the work for the service of the temple of the LORD is finished."

1 Chronicles 28:20 NIV

"Humble yourselves, therefore, under God's mighty hand, that he may lift you up in due time. Cast all your anxiety on him because he cares for you. Be alert and of sober mind. Your enemy the devil prowls around like a roaring lion looking for someone to devour."

1 Peter 5:6-8 NIV

NOTES

NOTES

Seasons of Transitions

A NECESSARY GROWTH

Our lives are compiled of a consistent flow of transitions. It might be the most visited season of them all. We experience transitions as we grow, learn, and keep taking steps forward into the next big thing.

Some transitions are exciting. Such as transitioning from high school to college, or into your first full-time job, getting married to your soul mate, or having your first child. But not every transition that you experience will contain excitement. Transitions are sometimes more worrisome and it can be stressful.

We don't always get the privilege of knowing what we are transitioning to. Like the transitional pull before the birth of a ministry, or the transition of growth in our walk with God. Those transitions try your trust and faith in God, which isn't always easy.

All transitions are uncomfortable, even the ones that have more exciting tones. But Friend, transitions are necessary for growth. If you were to take the growing pains of transitions out of the pace of life, it would take away our greatest opportunity of growth. If you aren't transitioning into something new, you will forever stay in the same place—likely dormant and stagnant in your walk with God and your career. Transitions can feel evil, but it's a necessary evil. It is essential to your growth in every aspect of your life.

This week, I pray that God gives you a wave of peace over the stress of the transition you might be going through. I know they aren't always joyful, but they come to be when the transition is complete. You just have to remember through this process, that you can always find constancy with Him.

It's easy to get lost in the transition of change when nothing feels stable or certain. But God is always constant in His love, provision, peace, and compassion. It is crucial in this time that you rely on His unchanging nature, especially when your emotions are equally in a jumble like your life in the state of transition.

When you feel like you are being swallowed by the waves of transition, take a deep breath, and remember that this is just a pain associated with growth. God has you in His palm, and it's ever-stable.

"And the LORD, he [it is] that doth go before thee; he will be with thee, he will not fail thee, neither forsake thee: fear not, neither be dismayed."

Deuteronomy 31:8 KJV

"Trust in the LORD with all thine heart; and lean not unto thine own understanding."

Proverbs 3:5 KJV

"I am with you and will watch over you wherever you go, and I will bring you back to this land. I will not leave you until I have done what I have promised you."

Genesis 28:15 NIV

THE MOVE

Has God prompted you to move into a place, and you don't know where you are going? A place between here and there. A place that feels like anything but peace, stability, and fulfillment. It's a little place called transition.

Transition is simply the movement between point A and point B. But the chaos of this unknown change can throw your emotions into believing you have lost your pace of normalcy and sometimes, your purpose.

At point A, you have a promise, then point B is the fulfillment of that promise. It's that unforeseen time in between that causes us to lose ourselves in incompleteness. That sense of incompleteness can cause a myriad of negative feelings such as loneliness and feeling like there is no place for you.

Transition has a funny way of separating you from what's toxic. Such as relationships, activities you're involved in, and skewed beliefs about yourself. This separation is the chaotic blow that makes everything appear unstable.

But in all this chaos, we have to remember that the movement, change, and separation is not a punishment or a wrong decision on your part. But it is a necessary hardship to allow you cross the threshold from transition into point B.

You cannot live in point B the same way you have been living in point A. The Bible says in Psalms that the deep calleth unto the deep. At point B, we have a new weight of responsibility in our prayer lives, in our sacrifices, and in our walk with God. What felt fulfilling for you at point A will not be sufficient for you at point B.

In your time of transition, God prepares you for the things that are to come. He will grow you into the person you are meant to be and equip you with the strength necessary for the weight of the promises.

A few things to remember in a season of transition: Keep moving even if you don't know where you are going. Stopping in a season of transition will only force you to live in a dry place below the blessings and prom-ises God has for you. Secondly, trust Him. In all things, trust Him. You may not know where you're going, but He does.

You will live to see point B Friend. Just keep moving forward. Keep trusting. Keep reading. Keep praying. Keep going to church. Your promise is coming.

"By faith Abraham, when he was called to go out into a place which he should after receive for an inheritance, obeyed; and he went out, not knowing whither he went."

Hebrews 11:8 KJV

"By faith he sojourned in the land of promise, as in a strange country, dwelling in tabernacles with Isaac and Jacob, the heirs with him of the same promise:"

Hebrews 11:9 KJV

UNROOTED

If I could pinpoint in a few words what my season of transition felt like, it would be uprooted, unanchored, and displaced. This, coupled with the emotional weight of its duration caused a very hurtful, lonely, and faith shaking season.

Harder than not knowing what I was transitioning into was feeling like home was no longer home. Friends weren't very close, and family seemed scattered. My singleness was another stab to the emotional feeling of being unanchored.

Whether you can identify it or not, the only constant thing in life is change. Things are being uprooted, moved around, and running in different directions. Some people are good at rationalizing these emotions accompanying change. But the longer things linger in a state of upheaval, the harder it becomes to find a purpose in your season.

Friend, I know how hard and emotional it is to feel like you don't have a place. Feeling uprooted is a special kind of grief. I can't promise you that this season will end soon, but I can tell you that you have a place, you have a purpose in this season, and you are most definitely not alone.

You know, sometimes (most times) when we get a feeling of being unrooted, God is prompting us to plant our roots firmly in Him. He shakes things up to show us that He can calm things down. He reorders, realigns, and when things start to come back into order, it will be better than what we could possibly imagine. It is hard to see while things seem to be in utter turmoil, but that's where our faith comes into play. To survive a time of being unrooted, you must cling on to a hope, a promise, or a word even if you don't believe its validity yet.

I know things are unsteady right now, but remember, He is your anchor, your rock to stand on when the winds of change are threatening to knock you off your feet. You may not be certain of a lot of things right now, but one thing that you can be certain of is that He is the unchanging factor in every changing aspect of life.

In your unsteadiness during this season, stand firmly on the truth that you always have a place with Him.

"For our citizenship is in heaven, from which we also eagerly wait for the Savior, the Lord Jesus Christ,"

Philippians 3:20 KJV

"And we know that all things work together for good to them that love God, to them who are the called according to his purpose."

Romans 8:28 KJV

"In my Father's house are many mansions: if it were not so, I would have told you. I go to prepare a place for you."

John 14:2 KJV

THE TRANSITION CALLED PREPARATION

Ever since I was a little girl, I have always heard that I have a great purpose. One of which is beyond my wildest hopes and dreams, and unlike anything that has so far been seen.

If you grew up in church and actively pursuing the things of God, you may have heard similar things. But for me, even as a little girl, I held tight to those things I perceived as promises from God even though I didn't know what it meant or that it might not even be true.

I will be transparent and tell you; this promise has been hard to hold onto because of insecurity, circumstances, and skeletons that had to be dealt with for me to move on. But none of these things challenged my faith harder than a year-long season of transition.

I don't (and perhaps never will) have the pieces of this grand plan put together. All I knew then was that He was transitioning me. But instead of gaining friends, confidence, and connecting with people, I became separated from those closest to me, fearful of the future, and insecure about what I believed.

A season of transition quickly became a season of struggle to feel wanted or needed. I felt the opposite of what I thought I should have been feeling. I felt unloved, forgotten, unequipped, incapable, and worst of all, separated from God. I was doubting, and my faith started to crumble.

I realize this short biography will not relate to everyone reading this devotion. But I would be amiss if I did not recognize those who become lost and sometimes forgotten in the transition season. Friend, if this is relatable to you, I just want to remind you of a few things...

God has not changed His mind about you. Even though you might be in a dry isolated place, don't let what you see absorb what you know, and what God has said about you. You are not alone; God's ways are not our ways. They are higher and greater.

The unawareness of His will can be blinding and hurtful. But if we are anchored to the Rock who is faithful to lead us into higher places, we can do anything but fail. Don't be deceived by what you may see and feel right now. You will see the fulfillment of your promise and ministry. It's closer than it seems, and He is closer than you think. Just hold on a little bit longer.

"He staggered not at the promise of God through unbelief; but was strong in faith, giving glory to God; And being fully persuaded that, what he had promised, he was able also to perform."

Romans 4: 20-21 KJV

"Hear my cry, O God; attend unto my prayer. From the end of the earth will I cry unto thee, when my heart is overwhelmed: lead me to the rock that is higher than I. For thou hast been a shelter for me, and a strong tower from the enemy."

Psalm 61:1-3 KJV

THE THING ABOUT HURT

In seasons of transition, there can be a lot of unknowns. A lot of unknowns can begin to breed hurt.

The thing about hurt is, it hurts. It's painful, uncomfortable, and overwhelming. When you are in pain, you tend to be more sensitive, less trusting, and way more cautious.

Hurt makes you motivated and angry, or it makes you isolate and cut ties. Hurt makes you fly, or it makes you fight. It's a natural human response.

But in the midst of this "natural human response" hurt feels anything but natural. Hurt hurts.

I don't know what kind of hurt you are dealing with, but I understand what deep hurt feels like. I call it "soul hurt" or "soul pain." Soul pain is when it doesn't just affect your feelings; it affects who you are, what you believe you are, and who you believe you belong to.

There can be thousands of things that can cause that kind of pain. And I have felt it more than once. So has many other individuals walking around in masks who want you to believe they are okay. Hurt may have different influences and circumstances but hurt is universal. Hurt hurts.

The greater the hurt, and the longer you are swept off of your feet by the blow, the quicker you become bitter and permanently angry. Let me tell you; bitterness is harder to get rid of than it is to deal with the hurt.

Friend, others don't see the wound on your precious spirit, but God does. He knows exactly how wide and deep this hurt is. He is the physician to help you with your soul pain.

I know this pain has messed with your mind and has made you question your morals. Even bigger, I know how this hurt has potentially altered your view about God. But if you can't receive these words from anyone else, receive it from someone who knows and has been in the same predicament with you.

You are not alone; God knows the challenges you are facing. He hasn't left you to bleed out on His table. Trust His process. Trust His will.

You can put stock in the fact that He will take care of your every hurt. But you also need to put some stock in your strength and decide, will you fly or will you fight?

Will you choose faith instead of feelings? Will you choose Godly community over isolation? Will you choose to continue to hurt, or will you continue to heal? Will you stay in the fight, or walk away from the faith? Don't give this pain more access to your spirit than it deserves. You are worth healing, you deserve peace of mind.

It's up to you sweet Friend. You have an angelic support group and a crowd of fellow souls that have been healed cheering you on. You are still loved, you are still noticed, you are still chosen, and you are not alone.

"For I know the thoughts that I think toward you, saith the LORD, thoughts of peace, and not of evil, to give you an expected end."

Jeremiah 29:11 KJV

"For I reckon that the sufferings of this present time [are] not worthy [to be compared] with the glory which shall be revealed in us."

Romans 8:18 KJV

NOTES

NOTES

Seasons of No

SEPARATION

As you go through life the "no's" you experience will be endless. I'm not just talking about a denial to a question, but situations of "no." We experience many of these situations, although we may not realize it. Some of which are loss, rejection, loneliness, disappointment, and Godly separation.

Yes, you read that right. Separation ordained by God. In a season of separation, it can feel like a desert. And if you aren't careful, you may feel overrun by the emotions convincing you that you're alone.

What makes things harder is being proactive to stay connected. But instead of connection, you get a pushback that says *no*. Relationships become harder to maintain. And you may not be able to connect in ministry, despite your best efforts. It can feel like such a heartache and the hardest attack on your purpose.

I want to let you know that this season of separation is not a punishment. You didn't do anything to make God decide to throw you away. I dare to say you can rest assured that you are doing *something right*.

The simple explanation of why you are finding yourself in this season is because God is trying to pull you closer to Him. He is trying to show you that He is all you need to survive. He is your Friend, your Father, and your reason for ministering. He is trying to show you that you can find safety, assurance, and peace dwelling in Him.

It can be hard to shift your thinking into these positive thoughts when separation has warped your mind into thinking He is the bad guy. To conquer the intense emotions associated with this season, you must remember what He has done for you. Stop looking at the desert in front of you and remember where He has brought you from.

Don't get discouraged, and don't let the desert start tricking you out of the truth. You have a purpose. You have a place. You have a ministry. God loves you deeply. You won't be in this separation season forever. Keep your head up, trust Him, and trust His process.

"They did not say, 'Where is the LORD Who brought us up out of the land of Egypt, Who led us through the wilderness, Through a land of deserts and of pits, Through a land of drought and of deep darkness, Through a land that no one crossed And where no man dwelt?'"

Jeremiah 2:6 KJV

"For he shall be like the heath in the desert, and shall not see when good cometh; but shall inhabit the parched places in the wilderness, in a salt land and not inhabited. Blessed is the man that trusteth in the Lord, and whose hope the Lord is. For he shall be as a tree planted by the waters, and that spreadeth out her roots by the river, and shall not see when heat cometh, but her leaf shall be green; and shall not be careful in the year of drought, neither shall cease from yielding fruit."

Jeremiah 17:6-7 KJV

LONE VESSEL

It's funny, isn't it? How you can be in a room surrounded by people yet feel very lonely. It's one of those common paradoxes. There are numerous triggers that fling us into seasons of loneliness, such as a death, a failed relationship, or a move.

Whatever the reason or trigger, walking through a season of loneness is a difficult "no" to live with. When you are not careful, loneliness can feel like a direct attack on your joy.

Even David felt the pain of loneliness. He describes his season in Psalm 102, "For my days are consumed like smoke, and my bones are burned as an hearth. My heart is smitten, and withered by grass; so that I forget to eat my bread... For I have eaten ashes like bread and mingled my drink with weeping" (Psalm 102:3-4 & 9).

David was heartsick because of loneliness. He lost his appetite and shed many tears. But despite his internal brokenness, David didn't let his fragile emotions drive him to a place of bitterness. He communicated his pain to the Lord. Instead of blaming Him for the pain, David chose an attitude of truth and reverence. "But thou, O Lord, shalt endure forever; and thy remembrance unto all generations" (Psalm 102:12).

He has a plan, and He knows where you are. He is waiting for a lone vessel to draw near to Him so that He can use it to its maximum potential. He wants you to pour out your hurt to Him. But be mindful of how you approach your hurt just as David did.

> *"I am broken, but you can put me back together. I am emotional, but you created these emotions so that I might have a closer relationship with you. I feel like you have abandoned me, but according to your word, you will never leave me."*

He is faithful to hear your cry, and faithful to take into account your pain. Your willingness to be the lone vessel in His presence is the key that will unlock the next crucial step in the staircase of your purpose.

"When the Lord shall build up Zion, he shall appear in his glory. He will regard the prayer of the destitute, and not despise their prayer."

Psalm 102:16-17 KJV

"Let your conversation be without covetousness; and be content with such things as ye have: for he hath said, I will never leave thee, nor forsake thee."

Hebrews 13:5 KJV

"For our light affliction, which is but for a moment, is working for us a far more exceeding and eternal weight of glory."

2 Corinthians 4:17 KJV

HURTFUL DISAP-POINTMENT

How many times in a day do you get disappointed? You might be taking life by the horns, but the reality for some is living in a continual disappointment. Disappointments from others, yourself, and God, especially when He doesn't answer your prayers the way you planned for them to be answered. It's easy to excuse human disappointment because of our humanity, but harder to excuse God because He isn't human. He's God.

In our human nature, it's easy to blame our disappointments on His answers because of His deity. Let's squash that misconception now. He doesn't respond according to the merit of our actions, He responds according to His will. And just like our earthly father tells us "no" for the benefit of our safety, so does our Heavenly Father. Hurtful disappointment is an inevitable and necessary component of our growth.

For the record, it is okay to be disappointed. So don't feel condemned for feeling human emotion. It's also okay to talk to Him about it. Yes, He is a deity, but He robed Himself in the flesh so He can relate to how you feel in times like this. He came here to endure disappointment Himself so He could fully know the sting of this emotion. His mission is not to push you away from Him but to draw you closer, to keep you safe, and for you to dwell in His safety.

He would rather you yell at him in hurt then turn away in bitter silence. He is understanding, patient, merciful, comforting, and a grace-giving God. He never promised us a specific answer, but we are safe in the vein of His will if we can endure some disappointment. Don't be so quick to judge His motives because of how you feel. Your feelings are real and justifiable. But often, they lead you in the wrong direction.

In every disappointment that may have hurt you, remember that He loves you. His love is what dwells among us. His love is why He died for us.

Soon and very soon, this hurt will be worth it. Trust His will, because it will always be better than what we can come up with!

"And we know that in all things God works for the good of those who love him, who have been called according to his purpose."

Romans 8:28 KJV

"For he knoweth our frame; he remembereth that we are dust."

Psalm 103:14 KJV

"Trust in the LORD with all your heart and lean not on your own understanding; in all your ways submit to him, and he will make your paths straight."

Proverbs 3:5-6 NIV

A Hard No

I remember exactly every single detail about that particular day. I went downstairs to the dining table and sat down to eat. One bite in, the news I had been avoiding yet anticipating arrived. One of my mentors, someone who had been a mother to my whole family, passed away in the earlier hours of that day.

Stunned, I left my breakfast on the table with an appetite far gone. I walked calmly (in what felt like slow motion) to my room. I didn't cry, I didn't scream, I didn't have a meltdown. But I sat confused and deeply hurt thinking about the powerful prayer meeting we had just a few days back. Everything about this loss that I experienced made no sense.

I am not an expert on grief in any form or fashion, but this was the first hurtful loss that I had experienced. This was the loss that taught me how to grieve. It was also the first time I received such a hard, permanent and heartbreaking "no." I didn't know how to respond, what to say, or how to think.

If you are experiencing a loss, I know how you feel. It's one thing to receive a "no" from a parent as a child. It's another thing to be given a "no" from God with little understanding. In the death of a mother, father, child, friend, sibling, mentor, we look to Him with the same broken question, "why God?" Often we tend to respond with a backlash of bitterness.

It's hard to understand, but God always has us in His best interest. In the middle of a "no" season, it is important to remember that our God is not a no God. We must trust what He is doing, even when it hurts. Our adversary loves to twist things about God in the midst of traumatic situations. It is important to know in this season that He is a yes God. Yes to hope, peace, healing, love, comfort, freedom, deliverance, and yes to an expected end.

It is okay to be hurt and upset during this fragile time. The thing about this hard no is to learn how to grieve, but not to get bitter, to mourn without being thrown into depression and to question without faulting God for His will that we do not understand.

Though you may be walking in the shadow of death, you can rest your mind on the fact that He is closer than ever before, binding up your wounds, and bottling your tears. He knows where you are, and He has not forgotten you. You may not feel it now, but there will be victory at the end of this season.

"He heals the brokenhearted and binds up their wounds"

Psalm 147:3 KJV

"For I know the thoughts that I think toward you, saith the LORD, thoughts of peace, and not of evil, to give you an expected end."

Jerimiah 29:11 KJV

"He will wipe every tear from their eyes. There will be no more death or mourning or crying or pain, for the old order of things has passed away."

Revelation 21:4 NIV

"Blessed are those who mourn, for they will be comforted."

Matthew 5:4 NIV

QUESTIONING

One of the most taboo discussions/prayers are those in which we question God. In our view of His power and greatness, we tend to feel hypocritical and awkward to ask God these hard questions. We are fearful even. Fearful of an angry response, fearful that we will get answers in a way that will further hurt us. Or worse, no response at all.

When we are in the middle of experiencing death or loss of any kind, it's hard to talk to the one who caused the hurt. It's hard to face that individual that hurt you. It feels like a deeper personal hurt when the 'individual' is God. But oh, how easy we forget the peaceful, healing, and preserving nature of God in the midst of negative circumstances. How quickly we forget that we are made in His image and likenesses. He experiences and feels all the emotions we feel.

He will not shun or condemn you for asking questions you can't grasp at a bit of its purpose. He wants us to ask Him the hard questions. He is excited to have the opportunity to answer, even though it may not be the way that we want. As a father answers the disturbing questions that plague the mind of his child, so is He with us. His shoulders are big enough to hold your emotions, and He is patient enough to give you time to process His answer.

Friend, it is okay. Ask your questions, express your feelings, process His responses, but don't forget to be still enough to hear His whole answer. If you are intent on listening, He will whisper a reassurance, unlike what humans can give. Yes, He is the taker of life, but just as easy as He takes life, He breathes life quick and easy. Let Him breathe life back into your situation, even if you don't understand.

He loves you; He has not forsaken you, He still holds the whole world in His nail-scarred hand.

"And we know that in all things God works for the good of those who love him, who have been called according to his purpose."

Romans 8:28 KJV

"Let us therefore come boldly unto the throne of grace, that we may obtain mercy, and find grace to help in time of need."

Hebrews 4:16 KJV

"Behold, he that keepeth Israel shall neither slumber nor sleep. The Lord is thy keeper: the Lord is thy shade upon thy right hand. The sun shall not smite thee by day, nor the moon by night. The Lord shall preserve thee from all evil: he shall preserve thy soul. The Lord shall preserve thy going out and thy coming in from this time forth, and even for evermore."

Psalm 121:4-8 KJV

SEASONS OF NO

For the last day of this last week of this devotional, I decided to include my first spoken word written and performed. I wrote this out of a personal, very hurtful no in my life, but out of this pain birthed the concept of this book and those to follow. I pray that God will give you peace and bring you comfort not just in your season of no, but in all of your seasons.

To everything, there is a season, and a time to every purpose under heaven... seasons to sew, seasons to reap, seasons to cry, seasons to laugh, seasons of torment, seasons of peace, seasons of pain, seasons of healing, seasons of 'yes', and even seasons of 'no.'

We jump at the opportunity to dance, and shout, and sing in our seasons of yes. But it becomes a different story when God decides to say "no."

But even if you are in a season of "no," it doesn't disqualify the perfection of His will.

A healing that never came does not make Him any less of a healer. For what He doesn't heal here, he makes whole there.

An unpaid bill doesn't make Him any less of a provider, rather He is just being creative in the process of your provision.

A prodigal resisting the pull from your prayers doesn't mean He is blind to your request rather He is crafting a greater testimony.

Even the most popular in the Bible had seasons of "no."

The Israelites roamed for 40 years.

Joseph was thrown into another prison.

Naomi became Mara

The prodigal ate pig slop.

And Lazarus died.

But in the face of silence, bitterness, desperation, death, and painful "no."

The Israelites arrived at the promised land.

Joseph became pharaoh's right-hand man.

Naomi became a part of the bloodline of Jesus.

The prodigal son came home.

And Lazarus walked out of his grave.

So in the midst of your season of no, Don't let condemnation turn His holiness into intimidation. Don't let fear dictate your faith. Don't let mistakes position your future. Don't let earthly pleasure blindside your sacrifices. Don't let pride control your feelings. Don't let bitterness steal your joy. Don't let the "no" hinder your praise.

He was and is and will forever be in any season, Jehovah Jireh, our provider. Jehovah Rapha, our healer. Jehovah Shalom, our peace. Jehovah Raah, our shepherd.

El Shaddai, El Elyon, Adonai. The most high God.

Be rest assured that His will is perfect even in your season of "no."

As Isaiah 55 says,

"For as the heavens are higher than the earth,

So are My ways higher than your ways,

And My thoughts than your thoughts.

"For as the rain comes down, and the snow from heaven,

And do not return there,

But water the earth,

And make it bring forth and bud, That it may give seed to the sower

And bread to the eater,

So shall My word be that goes forth from My mouth;

It shall not return to Me void.

Before you claim your justified feeling of pain, remember great is His faithfulness. True are His promises. Everlasting is His presence. And Perfect is His will.

HE sacrificed himself for a no season, only to be resurrected in every aspect of yes. Yes to hope. Yes to salvation. Yes to new life, yes to victory. In every season, in every storm, in every trial, He is the God of your no season.